Tomb

Nothing is as empty as the silence in my womb. However did a piece of me, become your body's tomb?

I wonder what I am supposed to do, with the parts of me I hate. Where do I put your tiny clothes? Your blankets? My heartache?

My body was meant to nurture you, make your heart grow strong. They speak of joy and nature's gift – they say nothing of what could go wrong.

I hate my body for letting me down, I will never trust it again. They ripped you out and put you on fucking machines – how was that going to make you mend?

In my life I had no room for error I was busy being mother and wife, how am I to be complete? That day will haunt me for my life.

How much more can I long for you and just what the fuck am I to do? Even when there's happiness there is not, for I always think of you.

I dream of your little precious face before my crying eyes. The ache just starts all over again. Fuck! Fuck! Fuck! Why did you have to die?

The urge I have to kiss your skin, hold and caress you in my arms; I wish my time over again; would five more minutes have done such harm?

I saw your face, a shock of dark hair and your perfect thin lips, hands soft and plump with flesh you looked doll-like when you met your death.

I speak and ask often if she felt peace in my stomach where she laid. Did she know that it wasn't going to last? That she wasn't going to stay?

Did she know how much we wanted her, the dreams that we had built? How many times I've gone over it all; that I am destroyed, racked by silent guilt?

Who could understand the things I do to survive my personal grief? I still search, I search for something? Anything? I beg for some relief.

It is dark and silent moments where I think of her the most. In my mind is where she grows old. She has to be mine to be with me. She is more than just my ghost.

I hope she liked her funeral; I hope she thought it nice. Since that day the thought of holding her has become my greatest vice.

And I pretend that she is with me I carry her every step I take, I know too well this is no dream from which one day I will happily awake.

Grief, it makes me lonely. It keeps me all alone. I feel like a tired and barren mother. I cling to the bond death brought us and secure it loyally to me – for each of us. For her and I, there is and shall be no other.

Tomb in Real Time

Nothing is as empty as the silence in my womb. However did a piece of me, become your body's tomb? *The walls and doorways blur past my head. I hear voices, no faces. What do they say? They are talking too fast.*

I wonder what I am supposed to do, with the parts of me I hate. Where do I put your tiny clothes? Your blankets? My heartache? *Smells weird I can taste it, "Sharon can you count backwards?" What? I am calm, aren't I? Can I count...... 10......9...*

My body was meant to nurture you, make your heart grow strong. They speak of glow and beauty; – they say nothing about the things that could go wrong. *Beep. Beep. Beep. Cords and noise and tubes, foreign pain, just weird, like a dream. Am I dreaming now?*

I hate my body for letting me down, I will never trust it again, they ripped you out and put you on fucking machines. This is to make you mend? *Can't get up. Surgery sore. Want to see my baby. Why isn't it okay? Where is it? "Is is a boy or a girl?" A girl! How wonderful. Can't stay awake... eyes are heavy.*

In my mind I had no room for errors I was too busy being a mother and a wife how am I ever to be complete? I will be haunted by that day for the rest of my life. *Crib all covered in machines. You're black. veins, transparent skin, no skin almost. I am scared. "Are you sure that's mine?"*

How much more can I long for you and what the fuck am I to do? Because even when there's happiness I always think of you. *Back to bed. It's touch and go, she is a very sick little girl. Rest is best now dear, just rest. I can't keep my eyes open. Close them, find somewhere peaceful and safe in the dark, there is nowhere. God, what is happening? Breathe.*

I dream of your little precious face, before my crying eyes and the ache starts all over again. Fuck, why did you have to die? *Sign the consent forms. Helicopter will transfer her; you will see her in a week. Tears. Tears. Tears. How can I cry so many bloody tears. Stop, fuck! Stop it all! Let me be! Somebody help me!*

The urge I have to kiss your skin and to hold and caress you in my arms - I wish my time all over again; would five more minutes have done such harm? *Red angry stitches welted across my belly, breasts sore with milk eyes swollen with tears, every bit of me weeps for you. A hurtful reminder that I am useless. You do not need me. I cannot help you live. I am useless.*

I saw your little face, head of dark hair and your perfect lips your hands had such soft plump flesh you really looked at peace when you met your death. *Fight everyone. Get moved beside you. Now I'm calmer. I just want to see you. Watch you breathe, watch the machine breathe for you. Sleeping upright at your crib. Once we were together again we remained that way. No more separation. Big lumpy grey recliner oh how I love you. My bed, my kitchen, my safety. My child. My child.*

I speak and ask her often if she felt peace in my stomach where she laid? Did you know that it wasn't going to last, that you weren't really going to stay? *Washing in the toilets. Freshen up to make it through each day. Only know to get up and start, stupid? It is *all I know, it is familiar. Stitches pull – infected, angry angry angry red line; looks how I feel .. ugly, ugly, ugly, sore, raw and very very wrong.*

Did you know how much we wanted you, the dreams that we had built; how many times I've gone over it all – racked by silent guilt? *Little dark room with too many chairs and hideous neon lights, the doctor talks in quiet and low tones. This calm voice is not my friend, his demeanour is soft yet his words are violent. Mean and hurtful. He is kind and gentle, he is braver than I. He says "Let me know after you have a talk to your family, it's a big decision for a Mum to make". I want my parents. So so so alone. I am alone. I am ruined. Nothing is ever ever going to be the same after being in that little neon room. I am fucked. I am defeated.*

Understand the things I do to survive what is my own personal grief and still I search for something. Anything. I pray for sweet relief. *Bathe you in your crib and dress you in a white cotton gown. Touch you and caress you, allowed to now, you are not removed from me. We drown you in love, talk to you about the future about to be stolen and silently I beg your forgiveness. I have failed, I have failed you and me, I have failed us all. It is a terrible feeling, one which I feel I will never escape? I turn the monitor off, no more beep, no more woosh, no more alarm, now we look for you to stop breathing. The tubes and lines are removed slowly, deliberately from all over you, we caress you, savour touching you as we work silently, sorrowfully. Now we watch you. Breathe my angel, breathe. I trick myself into thinking they are wrong, you will be the miracle. Breathe, breathe. Are you breathing? I breathe for you, I have never wished for anything as much in my life. Breathe, draw breath just once more. Please?*

In the dark and silent moments I think of you the most. In my mind is where you grow. You have to be mine to be with me; you are more than just my ghost. *You fit my arms, nicely tucked in? With your face looking up at mine. I drown you in my gaze; examining, remembering, mentally capturing and etching you in my mind. The morgue brings a quiet. Here with you motionless, here is a calm, I think it is insanity, I think I am lost of mind. My heart dictates everything, I am angry and yet when I hold you I know to be calm. I am maternal, hold you like a new born, wrap you, coo to you, lay you like a cherub. This is bliss. I hate to leave. At night I am terrorised, I picture you alone in a cold morgue fridge waiting for the box. You must be scared? I am. My mind will not escape this thought. I am exhausted, I can only fret at these feelings. I am useless.*

I hope you liked your funeral I hope you thought it nice because since then the thought of holding you has become my greatest vice. *I am alone. surrounded by people, by love and yet I just need to be alone. I nurse you through the service. I am so happy, so happy. You are here, I am here. Leave us be, just let it continue. I look up at the religious dude and hope he prattles on with his crap forever. He doesn't agree with me holding you at his sermon and nursing you whilst he extols Him as a way to explain this death; loving your cold dead body is easy, our time is running out. I don't care for the Minister's words. I am busy silently telling you the tale of my love. I lay you on the table with a pillow under your head, how pathetic and pointless, like you can feel anything now. Walk out legs, move for me, I shall not let them see me weaken. Be strong, don't. I don't. I can't look back. That cold moment was our longest embrace and our goodbye.*

And I know that you are with us; you are with me every step I take, I've learnt that this is not a dream of which one day I will wake. *I fold your things and place them in the wooden chest that they bought – funny how it is bigger than your little pink coffin. In here I hide the things that make me cry, make me sad. There is no joy in this journey.*

Grief makes me lonely it makes me alone I feel like a barren mother. I take our bond and keep it close – for each of us there is no other. *They pull the stitches, the pain it hurts – blood and milk is gone – dried up, dry. It is over. It is done. I am sentenced. I am done.*

Do you see it?

What is this belief that there is a moment to look at, look to, work towards?

It seems that we want to know. When, when is it happening?

Dying is quiet, the wailing for and from the dead—long gone.

Replaced. The syringe and its juice full of peace. One jab, and you feel more relaxed.

Enough jabs and we can kill you.

We don't call it that.

Pain management....................
and, when you ask, timidly "is it coming?"

the language spoken;

treatment
management
strategy
timetables
appointments

Hope, dreaming of futures. Don't say it out aloud - leave it silent. Unspoken. Cling. Cling to hope, of sorts.

But they say focus.... focus on the treatment.

Fix

fix

fix.

Never mind the discomfort. Never mind that each day you are a little less. A lot less. This is life? Well, to be fair they don't talk about life either.

Treatment
Well-being.
Improvement.
Remission,

remission.

Are these euphemisms?

Hard for the ears to hear otherwise.

What of you? Your need?.

You need;

the outcome

the anticipation.

Moments spent at a clinic –
desperate   mending   healing

pathetic.

Weak.

For what? For a few minutes more?

A few minutes more please.

It comes, let it wait.

Your terms.

You are tired

You hurt.

You ache.

I fear you have been tricked.

Subservient, no match for them.

And we both know that they are no match for "It".

Waiting. Speaking in riddles, in tongues foreign to our non medical ears.

Soft pink walls, scenes of beaches framed in wood a point to look at, divert your eyes from the sorrowful eyes of others.

Silent. Sshhh. As if the air is sucked away. Not sure where, but not here – restrictive and so, so silent.

Brave we are not. There is silent terror as to tomorrow?

Yet, no tears.

Ready, stoic.

You share fears with me in those pretty rooms of death. I am useless in my audience.

This one, this room, is yours.

burn

Can't sleep. My mind does hear you, crying, late at night and in the early early morning.

You sob for your future that is no more. You don't want to die. I DON'T WANT YOU TO DIE.

Head throbs with stress and the heart aches. Clutch chest – it still hurts. Thump it, beg it, stop aching, rest.

Toss and turn looking for comfort that will bring sleep. It does not come.

Beg my eyes, do not to let the sting of the tears spill over.

They are not obedient. They drop. And once they fall they will not stop.

Cry for you and cry for me. I feel your loneliness.

One thought keeps burning my mind. If you're not here then who am I?

We are entwined, like any father and child no doubt, but perhaps just a little bit more? I need it to be special.

We rage together. No words. Same mind, same type, same. Sarcasm and wit akin.

Intolerant and selfish. Mirrors.

It is a sickness to watch you diminish. Lessen.

Eyes dulling. Arms weakened and limp.

You can only squeeze me tight with the silent bond. No longer can I feel your wonderful strong embrace,

Oh how many months now since your flesh held my fears.

I always retreated there. Always sheltered there.

It is gone. Can't help but burn. If you're not here than who am I?

Decay

I see you eroding, disbelieving that this is real.

Where once I would curl up in your strong arms – there is now fragility.

I cuddle you up; –roll you into my arms.

Thinking this is how you must have always felt with me.

I wish to protect you, capture your breath and keep you enveloped.

My smell, My world.

Your body is failing you. Your scent has changed. Gone is the sweet, spicy cologne.

The smell of you that I sniff out in your wardrobe. Pillows where your black hair laid, chairs where your long legs stretched - seeking traces of you.

It has gone, I know not what minute it disappeared.

Like the tumour, it is insidious, it is stealing you from us one decaying piece at a time.

Your lips are different, your eyes dull. Where there was wit there is now apathy, vacancy in your eyeballs where green mischief used to live.

You do not rise to banter and in your very long everyday you rarely care for anything other than the pain of what is becoming you ...

killing you.

I am useless – helpless, hopeless. I resent the tears that burn the back of my eyes. I sneak into the bathroom and hide my sorrow.

I miss you. My arms ache for your skin. To be held in your embrace ... by you. To be able to put my conversation ...to you.

I long for your companion again.

I have not finished and the grieving has already begun.

This hurt is no stranger for me but I fear, like before, I will not survive it.

Your influence is great. You are my blood and my mind. Not just my physical body but my nature,

You are indeed an anchor for the violent temper and aggression; how ironic that you now bring this softness to my heart that I resent, that I detest.

I hate this weakness, the frailty catches me unawares.

Tears, where there is meant to be no emotion. Trails of thought that leave the sharpest conversations to wonder upon your health.

Shallow optimism that you will be better when I visit next ......

that you will be awake and mobile ...... able to talk through your discomfort.

How did we get here?

I shall seek your ghost. I seek it now looking, searching, yearning. I fear though that forever more it shall only live in a temple constructed in my mind. Oh, how my child cries for your very existence. I miss you already. I miss you now.

My Ilk

I wait for the pain to vanish, for the angst to submerge in my life.

And there is no end that I know of. The pain bleeds me out, a sharp cold knife.

I replay the moments over and over. I search for the hurt …..

it is my ilk.

The yearning I have to be with you is natural …

like mother's milk.

All of the choices I make are you; don't distinguish the good from the bad,

I wade through a haze just to clock over each day, there is nothing.

I am never nothing but sad.

And when I seek solace in the things that I do, no lasting joy to me appears.

For the torment is actually my mind; I see you there, you are the realisation of all my fears.

So I wait ... I wait ...

for forever will come to me, I've little respect for personal gains.

I have learnt that I will always sabotage my way in this life. Your death, my invisible emotional chains.

As I wander through endless darkness and beg to be set free.

I seek to find a place in my mind that is bliss, otherwise ...

how in hell will I ever find me?

Tired

To rest in arms

It is so lonely here inside my head,

I can't let you in and yet I can't seem to get out.

Sensitive is my body, a scab that won't heal, this grief, this horrifying grief threatens to consume me.

To be trapped in this world. I am scared.

Scared.

Where is my respite? Where is my sanity, where am I?

The compulsion to cry, to ache, to do harm is always at the fore.

I must push it down, keep it down or we won't survive it.

I won't survive it - I know for I've been to this darkness before.

I need calm, peace, denial; I need an alternate existence to this ache.

To remember, is to revisit, is to immerse myself, is to acknowledge, it is to forfeit unwillingly to sorrow.

Please, I can't. I don't want to hurt anymore.

Wrap me up in loving arms and keep me there even when I thrash violently against your concern, your care.

You need to know that I can't do it without you. If I am alone I will make my residence there.

Be still my tears...   breathe ... breathe ...

Breathe.

Breathe.

It is too much and yet never enough; I have suffered enough and then not nearly.

An end I seek; at the same time scared to find it, for you and I both know that while I am scarred I rage. And to rage is to live.

Better than the other option, isn't it?

Release me.

Release me pain. Release your strangling grip on my mind and my heart.

Breathe.

Breathe.

Calm down. Be still.

Rest. Rest in his arms. He is anchored. He shall keep you here. He shall keep you safe.

Don't worry; when you slide into the torment, he waits. Ever patient of things he does not know, cannot understand.

Be quiet.   Breathe.   Breathe.

Breathe out.

He will be there when we surface. He is true. He stays, even when he sees you eroding.

Rest now, we're tired.

I'm so tired.

dad

can't even contemplate it.
there is an anger that makes the tears hot
to my eyes.

to deny is the only way to function, yet the
mind knows. my mind knows that you are
going to die.

what will become of us? I have no energy to
fight this, no strength to face it.

confide in me your fears? do you see them
mirrored in my eyes?

I have not answers nor hope for you. just
love. and a longing for you to not hurt.

where is faith now? not mine of course but
yours.

I need to think you believe, all the years of
hypocritical Catholic fascination. let it not
fail you now.

if ever I wanted a thereafter it is now. how
truly absurd. I need it not for me or her;
but, for you I wish it to be.

in the absence of hope I treasure time and moments.

cakes for birth focus on you. around you. with you. savouring your cynical ways and your cheeky words.

drinking it in, like the alcohol haze you swam in all those years. this is my haze.

my fascination with death has been long. since her. it has awed me, wooed me, sometimes even comforted me. it has very nearly killed me.

now, though now it has tricked me again. back to the pain. no control over when there are tears.

sitting in the coffee shop with my lover enjoying a rainy Sunday and suddenly it is here. It overtakes me, the senses heighten and I feel the sting – I am pathetic and vulnerable.

it torments me, it is robbing you. owning you. taking you away from us. from me but maybe not to her. maybe it goes nowhere. maybe I am right?

I ache with anger at the thought of not being able to process it better.

sensibilities are often overcome with emotion. how insulting to you? how demoralising to me? I shall not talk of it.

shoving it down deep. eating it down. drinking it down.

whilst ever it is threatening me we are okay. it is when I forfeit. when you forfeit that we lose.

for that is the bit that no amount of reasoning settles. you are dying. and for that terrible truth I grieve.

I deny

I deny myself your company.

It is not that I don't miss you or long to find the calm,

it is just not available to me anymore.

Where once I could talk and lay without for hours seeking a solace of sorts,

I now rush and fumble to leave ;

as if to stay too long will bring it all to the fore once again.

And whilst time has healed, doubtless

I am not of strength to visit the memory once more.

I have no resilience to the feelings, the ache is still the raw, hard breaking ache.

The tears are still the howl of a stranger to my ears and the sorrow is so deep and so dark it threatens to consume me.

After all these years the clutch of that hand of grief is what I fear most.

A few times when it has caught me over the years, when I have allowed it to caress me the place that it takes me is terrible, it raises fear in me unlike I have ever dreamt or known.

No place for joy or laughter or love. It is another territory.

The loneliness I feel there still haunts my memory, my mind.

I thrive in solitude but, too much peace and silence and my mind drifts to the dark where my grief, my pain and my love for you live and prosper.

I'd have thought when my beloved dad joined you it might bring relief.

A sense of connection - a release.

I was so wrong.

In joining you he left me alone to navigate without his understanding of me,

the hurt of both losses is echoed where you lay.

It has certainly been many years now for us,

a routine never settled, a story never told, an emptiness worn with resignation.

feel me, know me, understand me. When you went, sensibility and reason went with you; love denied.

My love denied.

You are my beloved.

Happy Birthday

Change is movement. Swift and fast
a summer's warm kiss, a cold winter's blast.

It is you, the constant I have in my days,
other things waiver but the grief, well it stays.

From the moment we met, I was destined to alter, stoic from the start – your death has made me falter.

Wishing you away just denies me the pain,
I am not who I was. I am not the same.

The years have lapsed yet my emotions still raw, I crave to be whole. To long for you no more.

Inside I am shrivelled, protected tight like a ball, your name silent on my lips. My heart yearns your call.

Years and changes aside, our bind is still strong, unhealthily fed. I nurture this overwhelming wrong?

My frail heart lives wherever you are, like grief, I am near you, it never seems far.

So I wear my mourning blankie in the memory of your birth, it burdens me so heavily. Yet ... it is us, it is all we are now worth.

Companion

He wanders in and out of the shed. He doesn't look for him like he used to, as if he knows he has gone.

Now he waits patiently for her, she isn't home much anymore. When she is, she is sad.

He has tears welling in his eyes; they, her and him are mirrors in this way.

She talks out loud to the air, he just looks at her. Slowly wagging his tail. Chin rested on his tucked under paws. His eyes well up some more.

Footsteps are welcome – at least by him. Depends on whose they are, for her. Daughters make the lips smile. Others not so much. Leave her alone, don't you know she wants you all to go away. He is not here and without him she wants you all to go to hell.

For him there is always excitement at the chance of joy, voices, laughter. Even tears shared are better than silence and lonely sobs. He is happy now.

She yells at him. He is even happier – he senses her spirit, her old self – you know, the one that used to live here before. Before we started missing him. Before he died.

Perched on his lounge, blanketed down he watches. She cries. He is of no use, he wags his tail. Moves about – not too much though for fear she'll throw him out.

He watches. She is sad. He is sad. The same things happen as before, just without him. He is not in the old shed, sitting in the smoke stained chair and watching the tele.

He is not down the back, tinkering amongst the petrol fumed machines and the rusty tools.

He is not on the sun baked verandahs, not chatting to Dan or watching the neighbours.

Nobody bothers him now. Not that we know of anyway. He is gone.

She cares a little less now. Things aren't as important, he is not there to smell her shiny clean floors or like the simple meals she made for him.

What then is the point? She lives meagrely, partly due to necessity but mostly because she has little will to live. Nor does she wish to die, she just wants it as before.

Before the death.

He knows she needs comfort. He taps his eager little paws, over the clean wooden floors. He wants to please her somehow but he always manages to get in the way, in her way.

She doesn't mean to be joyless; it is just that he's not in the shed. She doesn't look so much anymore. She talks, yells mainly – she hates it hates it now he is dead. What is she to do now. It is weird, not as before. There is nothing left like before. Though she tries to make things the same, make things okay.

At night she sits in her couch and looks ahead, eyes well. Tears that can't be held any longer fall. She looks across at the little dog, he has tears in his eyes and she says as much to him as to Him, "I know George, I miss him too.".

Pilgrimage

I have made this pilgrimage many times.
Over months, into the years.

Through the gates and the manicured lawns unfold ahead.

The flagpole that bangs its chain rhythmically against the metal, bang... bang...bang.

I am weary; I sense the rise and fall of my chest, a sigh that makes me feel guilty.

The car turns the roundabout up the little rise to you. I am drawn to your site. to your side.

Gerberas orange, burnt like a summer sunset. Red poinsettias with green nondescript brush. Not pretty just existing. A soothsayer for the absence of you all.

You haven't changed. So many long and unreconciled years.

If I don't prepare myself I still get caught short with tears sliding hot from these aging weary eyes.

Digging at the edge of the grass, square and sharp lines.

Polish up the cloth, rub the paw, the face, the worded up chest. Words that don't mean so much now. Though once, so hard to fill a little bit of us into you. How to describe all that we felt. Hard to talk of what I lost.

Where are you? You are not in the flowers, nor the pebbles or succulents that survive in the dry brittle soil that lays over you.

You aren't sandstone or granite. Not the birds in the tree nor the cones that they discard, after chewing the husks.

I know you for how you make me feel. The ache in my chest. The strain of the eyes. The sobs that I never initially recognise. You are never here. You are not.

Like wind. Not to be seen yet, still a linger on my skin.

You have not a face to which I can close my eyes and picture. You are not how I once saw you real.

Can time really change everything except for the feelings? Is there nothing to do other than make the trip?

Back down the hill. Rubbish in hand ready to throw away. The red lidded bin looks out of place, upright and ugly amongst the view of flowers, lawn and roads.

The soft thud of the door. I hear the engine and hold my breath tight. Goodbye again. My life with you is full of nothing but goodbyes.

Fingers clasp mine, his touch brings me back. Always. He wisely uses his skin to speak to my heart, my sanity, my despair.

He brings my focus around ever so slightly. As we be, exist, together we start to talk of the outside, the world. The world outside the heavy cemetery gates. Our pilgrimage complete.

For now.

Again.

Song for the son

Where did you go when you left him? Did you know how alone he would feel?

Did your yearning for Betty take over? The pain of missing her all too real?

You made that son of yours an orphan. No matter the families that he had made.

He longed for the safety of a Mum and a Dad. He pained for a return to a lost childlike way.

It has changed him to be without you. Neither a phone call or train trip away.

I'm not sure that he knows just how deeply he aches. I love him, I acutely feel this pain.

His want for you must continue, if ever we are to have our time.

He hopes you found a way to fill your heart, and that you exist somewhere other than his mind.

Be well and be loved wherever you are, and know that he misses your love a lot.

In my arms is where his heartache can lie, he is my essence. He is never alone now, he has me.

Dane

A loss is only as great as the love it leaves behind.

The place where he lives, is deep inside your mind.

And when the years fall over and your memories aren't as strong,

If you thought you'd forget, sorry, you'd be wrong.

Your tears still fall as often as day becomes the night.

Reasoning the death of him will be your thankless fight.

Endless days all roll into one as you get on with life's chores,

But he is your heart and your mind, the mystery behind closed doors

The thoughts that you wonder, like how would he have grown?

What sports would he have played? What friends would he have known?

Would he have been a challenge? Would he have an angel face?

Or would he have teen attitude with dirty clothes all over the place?

How your life could be different? It would not be the same.

If only you could feel complete, if only he was more than a name.

Of course this can never happen, some things will never be.

Life's lessons have taught us.

It's all too real for you and me.

So picture him how you want. Make him as perfect as he can be.

I know he would have loved you, no other way will do,

He is Dane. He is your son.

He shall always live in you.□

Shelter There

Your days of fighting like a hell cat are over; or at least they are whilst ever you swallow that pill.

Whatever it has taken from you is nothing; nothing compared to the world it has opened up for you, to you.

Gone is the thirst for blood, the need to hurt, to scare, to kill.

You now see people, see faces, see friends.

The picture has been turned down on your violent actions; it is working for now.

Whilst ever you swallow that tablet down.

Don't abandon it. Don't abandon you; tears well in my eyes each time I think of the pain. You have been tormented.

This journey for us has been long and hard.

We have been insulated, keeping the world out - it does not understand;

they do not understand.

It is now in the moment we feel freer, calmer. These moments that we celebrate as accomplishments, others call them just routine.

I beg you. I beg you. I beg you.

Stay with the plan, it keeps you safe.

And for you my gentle lamb I always hope you shelter here in the tablets

whilst ever it makes you fight less I will be a fan.

I was... I am... Danny

I AM YOUR PARTNER, you've shone on my life;
our hearts are together – like husband and wife.
Promise not to cry for me all of your days and your nights;
I will always be with you – making sure you are alright.
Please feel my presence and please feel my love;
I am here. I surround you. I will watch you from above.

I AM YOUR BROTHER and will be for always;
I have shared in your life in many wonderful ways.
Please know I am with you, in one form or another;
look out for my daughter, take care of her mother.
Live your life to the fullest, it all lays ahead;
each day live a little for me and I will never be dead.

I AM YOUR SON, I hope I have done you proud;
remember all of the good times, not just this black cloud.
Please know it was not a plan, I did not choose to go;
but there are some things in life we just never know.
Be good to yourselves and all of those that I adore;
When your pain gets too much, I ask that you embrace them even more.

I AM YOUR FATHER, you are my every night and every day;
you are the twinkle in the stars, you are my precious sun-ray.
I trust you will be fine, you will grow stronger each year;
and with every breath you take, I hope to be near.
You will be surrounded by love, and by people who care;
and when you miss me the most, look deep inside – I will be there.

I AM YOUR FRIEND, we have shared life with laughter and tears,
may you talk of me often, I hope over a few cold beers.
Talk about how my life was good, how my life was strong;
focus on my achievements – not mourn the bits that went wrong.
Goodbye for now. Goodbye forever?
Goodbye to you I say.
I AM YOUR DANNY. I survive in you all, not in this coffin where I lay.

Searching

I see you, seeking, searching, looking.

Asking, pleading. Are they here?

You sense them, imagine them, long for them. You have broken your heart for me.

I am undeserving. Am I undeserving?

Is your joy worth the sufferance?

What amount is the toll? What price?

Am I worth it? Am I worthy?

Grieving can last for many years; a lifetime.

My heart hurts for you, for your sorrow.

There will always be the hope, the wish, the dream, the chance.

I am resigned.

Will there always be a hole?

Will our happiness be complete without their presence, their energy?

I sense you searching. I pray you find your bliss.

Buyer Beware

I am a wrecked and tortured beauty,

my scars are flaming red and raw – they are angry,

I've no real right to mate or couple up. It'll only end up badly.

The feeling one gets from heartache? Well it sits with me each day

I swallow the pain until it is my consuming core.

I am driven by grief, and it is best you stay away.

I may look like a trinket all shiny and desired.

But buyer beware because below the glossy sheen,

I am bitter and torn – a twisted old crone lives within.

I'm hard and sharp, my feelings are cool. I demand and I insist terribly.

My passion will devour everything it wants without favour and then;

well, then I move past you leaving you lost and broken as well. Buyer beware indeed!

I am not a toy to be trifled with nor a challenge for you to overcome.

I will be the end of many dreams and desires.

If you enter this space you better toughen up quick for the weak and the sweet will not survive here.

The Longest Apology

It has been the longest apology.

For near on two decades now I have offered you my sorry.

I have asked for you to forgive me.

I have been all of the blame and, I have been none.

My misery for the unfulfilled, the longed for, well, it knows no bounds.

I have only the notion of love.

The reality of it passed us by many, many, many moons ago.

Should there be others, should there be truth in the tales of faith?

Though I think not.

Then, I would hope that in these places, these moments that you may exist?

So long ago did I inherit this burden that I only vaguely remember the time when it did not sit within me.

And yet,

as heavy and as horrid as it is I take it and carry it, nurture it - for it is all I have of you.

For me it is you.

It is the sharp breathe, the throbbed heart, it is the sounds of sobs that escape me unrecognised as human, humane.

Ironic.

There can be no more a human sound than the mother's wail for the dead child.

Be it hollow, be it hard. If it is nothing, it is but real.

www.ingramcontent.com/pod-product-compliance
Lightning Source LLC
Chambersburg PA
CBHW022122090426
42743CB00008B/958